Ambulances

by Anne E. Hanson

Consultant:
Rob Farmer
Fire Fighter/Paramedic
City of Upper Arlington, Ohio Fire Division

Bridgestone Books
an imprint of Capstone Press
Mankato, Minnesota

Bridgestone Books are published by Capstone Press
151 Good Counsel Drive, P.O. Box 669, Mankato, Minnesota 56002
http://www.capstone-press.com

Library of Congress Cataloging-in-Publication Data
Hanson, Anne E.
    Ambulances/by Anne E. Hanson.
    p. cm.—(The transportation library)
    Includes bibliographical references and index.
    ISBN 0-7368-0841-8
    1. Ambulances—Juvenile literature. [1. Ambulances.] I. Title. II. Series.
TL235.8 .H35 2001
629.222'34—dc21   00-009954

Editorial Credits
Karen L. Daas, editor; Karen Risch, product planning editor; Timothy Halldin, cover designer;
    Erin Scott, illustrator; Heidi Schoof, photo researcher

Photo Credits
Daniel E. Hodges, cover
Lambert/Archive Photos, 12, 16
Leslie O'Shaughnessy, 8, 18, 20
North Wind Picture Archives, 14
Unicorn Stock Photos/Rich Baker, 4; Aneal V. Vohra, 6

1 2 3 4 5 6 06 05 04 03 02 01

Table of Contents

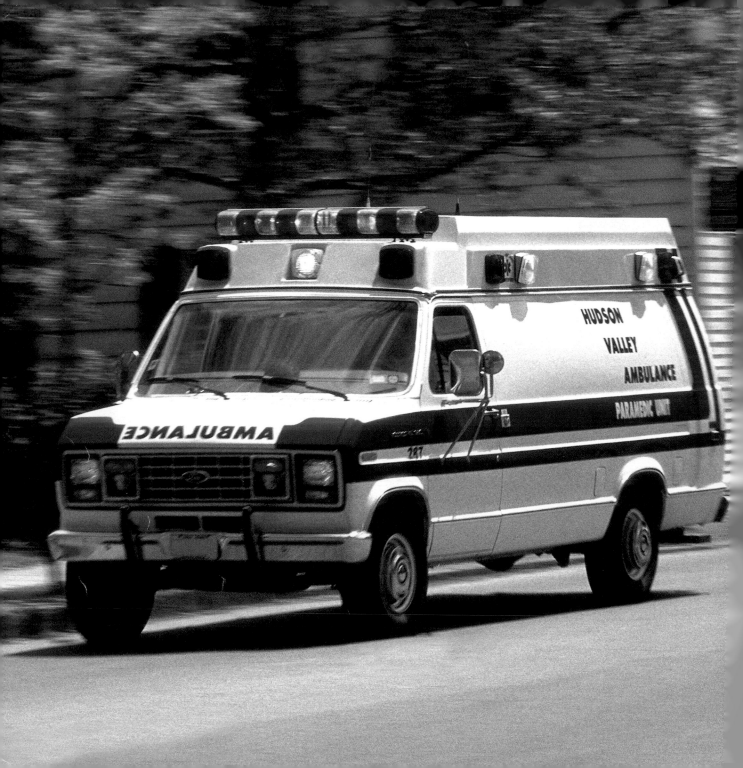

Ambulances

Ambulances rush sick or injured people to hospitals. Lights and sirens on ambulances warn drivers to move out of the way. Patients receive medical help on the way to the hospital. Ambulances help save lives.

patient

someone who receives medical care; EMTs and paramedics treat patients.

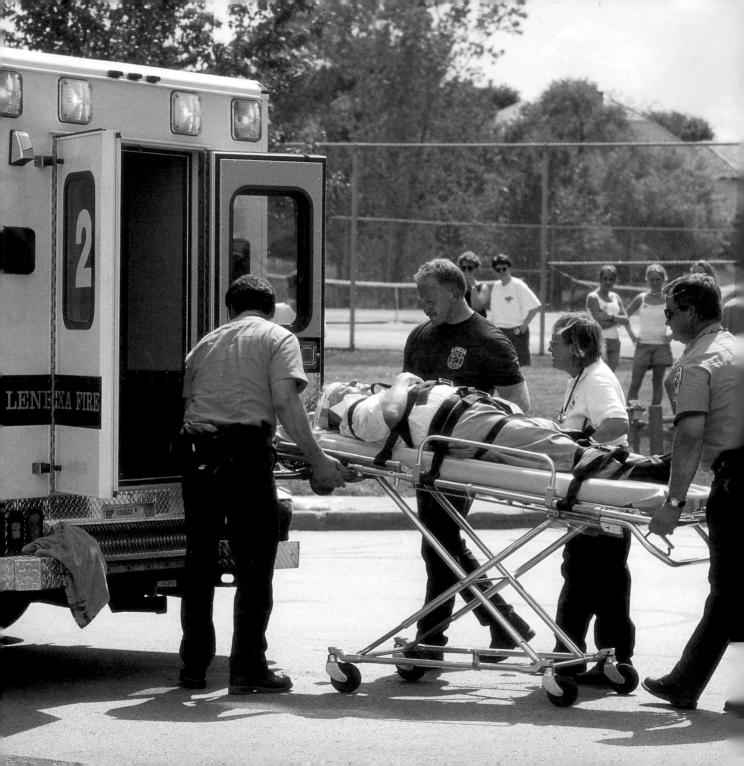

Ambulance Crews

Ambulance crews travel in ambulances. Emergency medical technicians (EMTs) and paramedics care for patients. Ambulance crews treat people in their homes or at accident scenes. They continue to give care as they transport people to hospitals.

accident

something that is not planned; people may be hurt in accidents

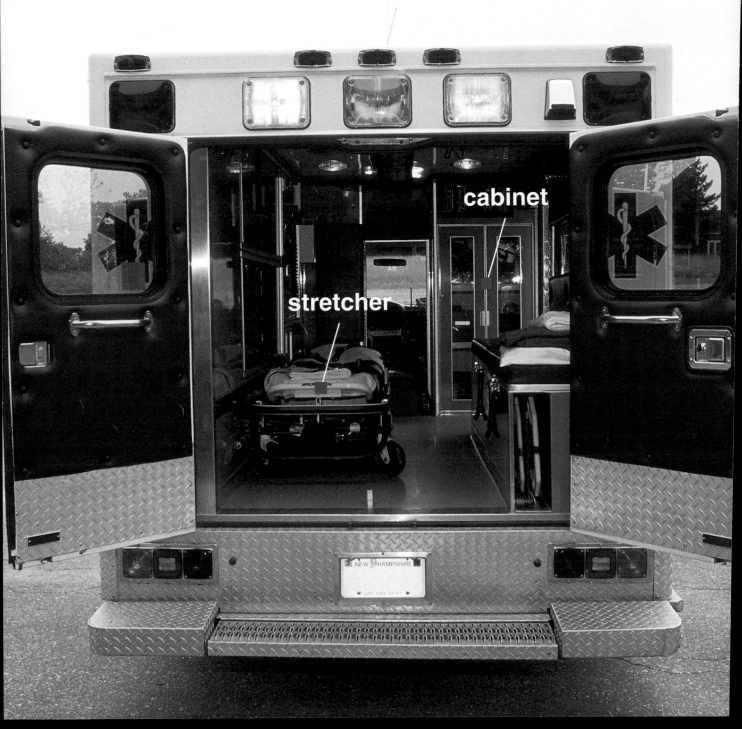

cabinet

stretcher

Inside an Ambulance

EMTs and paramedics care for patients in the back of ambulances. They may have the patient lie on a stretcher. EMTs and paramedics use medical equipment. They store the equipment in cabinets.

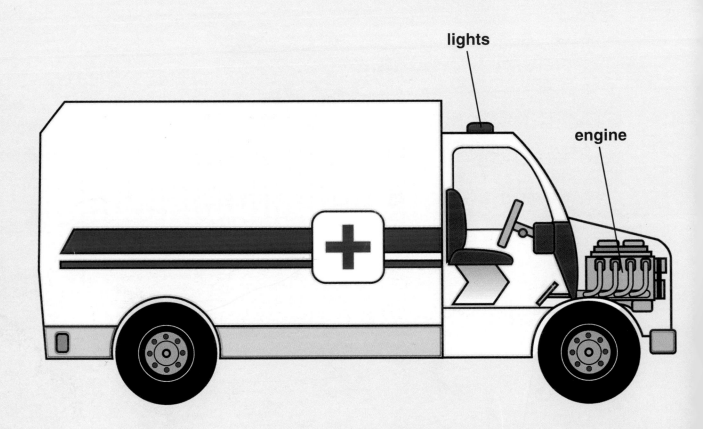

lights

engine

How an Ambulance Works

An ambulance has a diesel engine that runs on diesel fuel. The driver uses buttons to turn on the siren and lights. White lights help the ambulance crew see around the ambulance at night. Batteries power medical equipment.

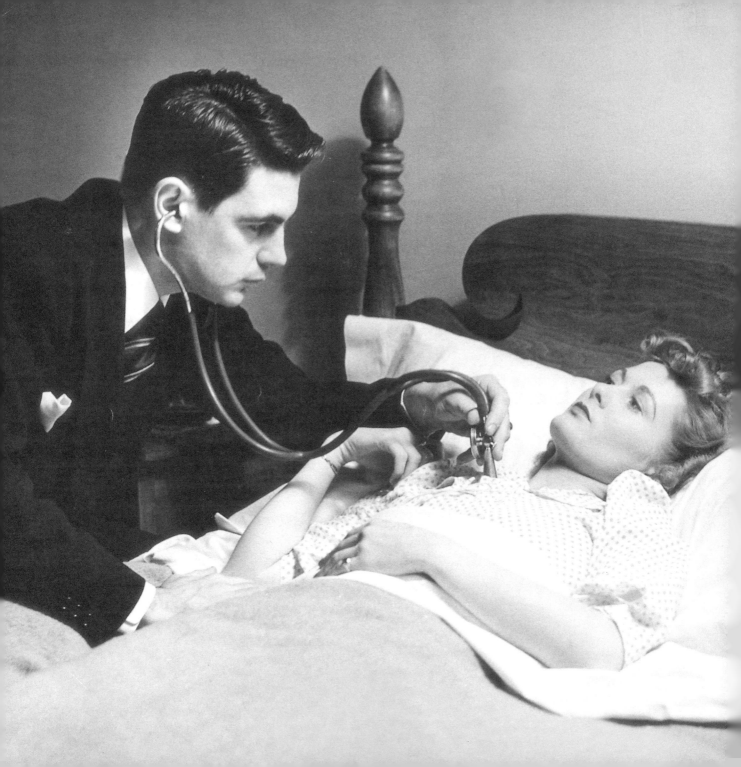

Before the Ambulance

Before the ambulance, many sick or hurt people did not get help quickly enough. Doctors walked or rode horses to homes. Friends or family members took sick people to the hospital. Wounded soldiers waited on battlefields for a nurse to reach them.

Inventor of the Ambulance

Baron Dominique Jean Larrey was a doctor. He invented the first ambulance in 1792. People called it the "flying ambulance" because it moved quickly. The horse-drawn cart could carry two people at a time. Many cities used ambulances based on Larrey's design.

Early Ambulances

Horses pulled the first ambulances. People on bicycles pulled other early ambulances. Later, people used large cars as ambulances. Many early ambulances did not carry medical equipment. They rushed people to hospitals for care.

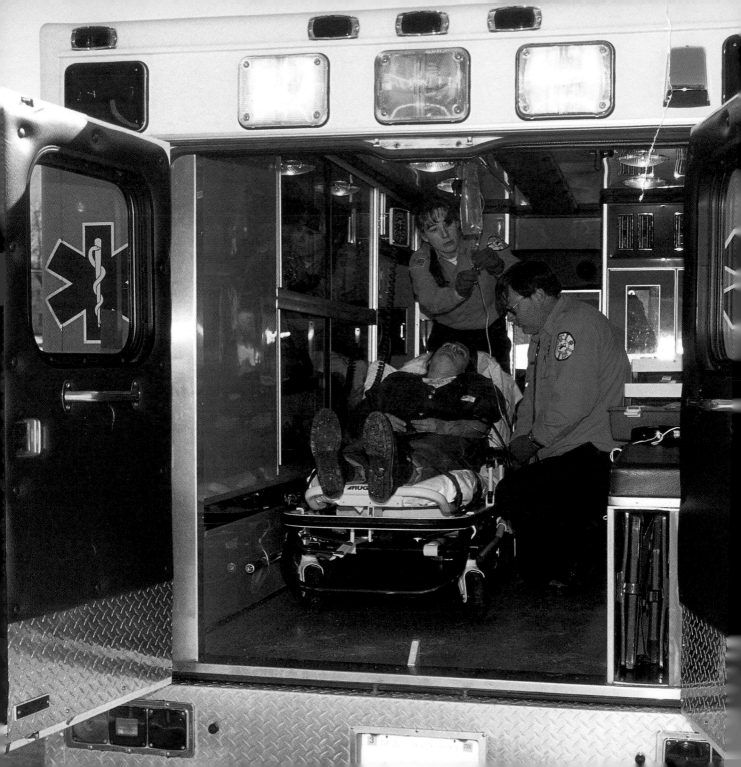

Ambulance Rescue Today

An ambulance crew hurries to help people during an emergency. The crew treats sick or injured people. They call the hospital. They tell doctors about a patient's injuries. Doctors and nurses are ready to care for the patient when the ambulance arrives at the hospital.

emergency
a sudden situation that must be handled quickly

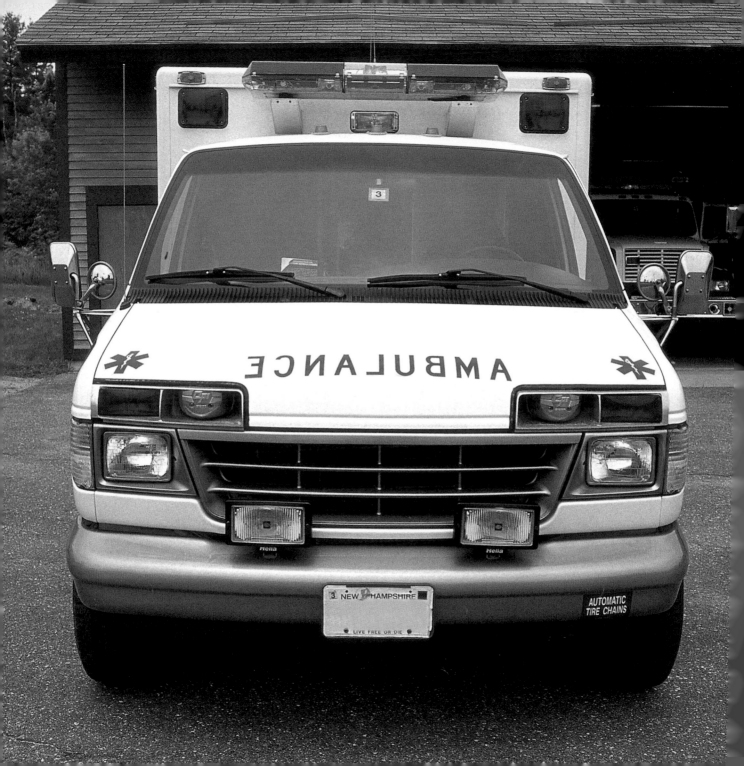

Ambulance Facts

- The word ambulance is printed backwards on the front of an ambulance. Other drivers can read this word in their rearview mirrors.

- Ambulances have big windows in back. The windows keep riders from getting carsick.

- Ambulances have crash bars near the bottom of the vehicle. These bumpers protect the ambulance in narrow areas such as alleys.

- The rear bumper of an ambulance flips down. EMTs and paramedics can then roll stretchers close to the ambulance. They can place the stretcher in the ambulance more easily.

Hands On: Check Your Pulse

EMTs and paramedics help people who are hurt. They check a patient's pulse to see how fast blood is pumping through the body. You can check your pulse.

What You Need

Watch or clock

What You Do

1. Gently place two fingers on the left side of your neck. You should feel your pulse. Your pulse throbs as your heart beats. Each beat moves blood through your body.
2. Look at a watch or clock. Count how many times your heart beats in six seconds.
3. Add a zero to the end of the number. This number is how many times your heart beats in one minute.
4. Run for one minute.
5. Repeat steps 2 and 3.

Your heart beats faster when you are active. It also beats more if you are scared or hurt. EMTs and paramedics can tell how fast a patient's heart is beating by the patient's pulse.

Words to Know

diesel fuel (DEE-zuhl FYOOL)—a heavy oil that burns to make power

engine (EN-juhn)—a machine that makes the power needed to move something

injury (IN-juh-ree)—damage or harm to the body

patient (PAY-shunt)—someone who receives medical care; EMTs and paramedics treat patients.

stretcher (STRECH-ur)—a piece of equipment used to carry someone who is sick or injured

transport (transs-PORT)—to move people or goods from one place to another

Read More

Bingham, Caroline. *Big Book of Rescue Vehicles.* New York: DK Publishing, 2000.

Mugford, Simon. *The Fantastic Cutaway Book of Rescue.* Brookfield, Conn.: Copper Beech Books, 1997.

Rogers, Hal. *Ambulances.* Rescue Machines at Work. Eden Prairie, Minn.: Child's World, 2000.

Internet Sites

Kid's Corner
http://www.rescue70.org/kids.htm
Safety City EMS Department
http://www.nhtsa.dot.gov/kids/ems/index.html
Toronto EMS—Just for Kids
http://www.city.toronto.on.ca/ems/kids/just_for_kids.htm

Index